FOR CHILDREN
AGES 5-11

STAY SAFE BE BRAVE!

A Guide to Personal Safety and Boundaries for Children and Caregivers

Created by Katherine Bluma

STAY SAFE BE BRAVE!

A Guide to Personal Safety and Boundaries for Children and Caregivers

Created by Katherine Bluma and Jewel Johnson

Stay Safe Be Brave!
A Guide to Personal Safety and Boundaries for Children and Caregivers

Authors: Katherine Bluma, Jewel Johnson.
Published by: My Success Strategist
Front and Back Cover by: Jewel Johnson
Copyright © 2024 by My Success Strategist

Created for Children Aged 5-11

Disclaimer: "Stay Safe, Be Brave" is an independent publication created to provide educational and informational resources for caregivers and children. While this activity book includes guidance on personal safety, body boundaries, and emotional expression, it is not intended as a substitute for professional advice, counseling, or intervention. The content, including activities, stories, and suggested resources, is provided for general informational purposes only.

We have made every effort to ensure the accuracy and relevance of the information presented, including references to support services and further education. However, the author and publisher do not guarantee the completeness, accuracy, or currentness of these resources. We strongly encourage readers to consult with qualified professionals and trusted organizations for specific concerns or situations.

The author and publisher disclaim any liability, loss, or risk incurred as a consequence, directly or indirectly, of the use and application of any content within this book. By using this book, you acknowledge that it is your responsibility to seek appropriate professional advice and to make informed decisions regarding the safety and well-being of the children in your care.

Dear Readers,

Welcome to "Stay Safe, Be Brave"—an activity book designed with one primary goal in mind: to empower children with the knowledge and confidence they need to protect themselves and respect others. Whether you are a parent, guardian, or trusted adult, this book is a tool for you and your child to explore together, helping to build a strong foundation in personal safety, body boundaries, and emotional understanding.

We understand that some of the topics and terms discussed in this book may be considered sensitive or uncomfortable for some readers. However, these conversations are crucial in ensuring that children are equipped with the tools they need to navigate the world safely. By addressing these subjects openly and honestly, we can help prevent potential harm and build a culture of respect and understanding.

For caregivers and trusted adults, this book also provides valuable resources and tips to support open communication about personal safety. We encourage you to use this book as a starting point for discussions that can continue long after the activities are completed. Your role in this journey is vital in ensuring that your child feels safe, heard, and respected.

Thank you for taking this important step with us. Together, we can empower children to face the world with courage and confidence, knowing they have the knowledge to keep themselves safe and the support of a trusted adult by their side.

TABLE OF CONTENTS

Dear Parents and Trusted Adults,

As we embark on this journey to help children understand their bodies and the importance of personal boundaries, it's crucial to recognize why these lessons matter so much. Educating children about their bodies and how to protect them is a vital part of ensuring their safety and well-being.

WHY TEACH ABOUT BODY BOUNDARIES?

EMPOWERMENT AND SAFETY

Empowering Children: When children understand their bodies, they gain confidence. This confidence helps them set and communicate their personal boundaries.

Recognizing Unsafe Situations: Knowledge about body boundaries helps children recognize when someone crosses a line, enabling them to respond appropriately and seek help if needed.

PREVENTION OF ABUSE

Awareness is Protection: Educated children are less vulnerable to abuse. They know how to identify unsafe situations and feel more empowered to speak up.

Speaking Out: Children who understand their boundaries are more likely to report inappropriate behavior to trusted adults, preventing further harm.

BUILDING HEALTHY RELATIONSHIPS

Respect for Self and Others: Teaching children about boundaries fosters respect for their own bodies and the bodies of others. This respect is foundational for building healthy relationships throughout life.

Understanding Consent: Learning about personal boundaries introduces the concept of consent, which is crucial for all interactions.

THE IMPORTANCE OF USING CORRECT ANATOMICAL TERMS

CLEAR COMMUNICATION

Accuracy Matters: Using the correct names for body parts (like penis, vagina, breasts, etc.) ensures clarity and prevents confusion. This accuracy is essential if children need to describe something that happened to them.

Understanding Across Cultures: Different families and cultures might use various terms, but it's important to have a shared understanding within your household.

REDUCING SHAME AND STIGMA

Body Positivity: Using proper anatomical terms helps children view their bodies as normal and natural, reducing feelings of shame or embarrassment.

Open Dialogue: Encouraging open discussions about the body helps remove the stigma that often surrounds these topics, making children feel more comfortable talking about their bodies.

AIDING IN EDUCATION AND HEALTH

Better Health Outcomes: Familiarity with anatomical terms aids in communicating health related issues accurately to doctors and healthcare professionals.

Lifelong Learning: Understanding their bodies is the first step in a child's journey toward learning about puberty, reproduction, and sexual health as they grow.

A NOTE ON CULTURAL SENSITIVITY

It's important to acknowledge that different cultures and families may use different terms for body parts, and that's perfectly okay. What matters most is that everyone in your family understands and agrees on the terms you use at home. Having a shared vocabulary helps avoid misunderstandings and ensures that everyone is on the same page.

HOW TO USE THIS BOOK

This book is designed to be a tool for both children and trusted adults to explore these topics together. Each section provides activities and discussions to help reinforce understanding and encourage open communication.

Engage Together: Use the worksheets to learn and talk together. Answer questions, share experiences, and build a safe space for discussion.

Set Family Guidelines: Agree on the terms you will use in your household and discuss what boundaries mean to your family.

Practice Safety Plans: Develop safety plans and practice how to respond if a boundary is crossed.

By teaching children about their bodies and boundaries, you're giving them the tools they need to protect themselves and build respectful relationships. Thank you for taking this important step toward your child's safety and empowerment.

Welcome to

"SAFETY FIRST: A Caregiver-Child Guide to Personal Safety and Boundaries"

This book will help you learn how to stay safe and feel confident. Let's have fun learning together!

NOTE TO PARENTS AND EDUCATORS

This book is designed to teach children about personal safety. Use it as a tool to discuss important topics and reinforce key messages. Our Goal is to encourage children to ask questions and express their feelings. At the back of the book there are resources for you along with exercises to reinforce what they are learning.

CHAPTER 1:
BOUNDARIES

Your body belongs to you, and you get to decide who can touch it and how.

It's usually okay to sit next to people, like your grandfather or your friends. Sitting next to someone is a nice way to be close without being too close.

But sitting on laps is different. It's okay to sit on mommy's or daddy's lap if you want to. But sitting on other people's laps, even family members or friends, can sometimes break safety and personal boundaries. It's usually better to sit next to them instead.

Remember, if you ever feel uncomfortable, it's okay to say 'no thank you' to sitting on someone's lap or even sitting next to them. You can always choose to stand or sit somewhere else.

If anyone ever makes you feel uncomfortable or asks you to keep a secret about touching, always tell me or [another trusted adult] about it.

Your feelings are important. If something doesn't feel right, trust that feeling. You can always come to me if you're unsure or if something happens that makes you feel weird or scared.

Certainly. Here's a simple, interactive exercise you can use to help children practice setting boundaries and understanding personal space. This exercise is called "My Space Bubble":

Materials Needed:
- A hula hoop or a piece of rope formed into a circle (about 3 feet in diameter)
- Optional: Some colorful stickers or markers

EXERCISE: "MY SPACE BUBBLE"

1. **Introduction:**
   Say: "We're going to play a game called 'My Space Bubble' to help us understand personal space and boundaries."

2. **Set up:**
   Place the hula hoop or rope circle on the floor. Have the child stand inside it.

3. **Explain:**
   Say: "This circle is your personal space bubble. It's the area around you where you feel safe and comfortable."

4. **Practice Scenarios:**
   Go through different scenarios, asking the child what they would do:
   a. Say: "I'm going to pretend to be different people. Tell me if it's okay for them to come into your space bubble."
   - "I'm your parent. Can I come in for a hug?"
   - "I'm your teacher. Can I come in to help you with your work?"
   - "I'm a stranger at the park. Can I come into your bubble?"
   b. For each scenario, have the child practice saying "Yes, you can come in" or "No, please stay outside my bubble."

5. **Role Reversal:**
   Let the child play different roles and you respond, reinforcing the idea that it's okay to say no.

6. **Discuss:**

   After the exercise, talk about:

   - How it felt to have control over their space.

   - Why it's important to respect others' space bubbles?
   - What to do if someone doesn't respect their bubble?

7. **Reinforce:**

   Say: "Remember, you can always say 'no' if you don't want someone in your space bubble, even if it's family or friends. Your body, your rules."

This exercise helps children:
- Visualize personal space
- Practice setting boundaries
- Understand that different relationships have different boundaries
- Feel empowered to say no to unwanted physical contact

Remember to keep the tone light and fun, but also emphasize the importance of the lesson. You can repeat this exercise periodically, adjusting scenarios as the child grows older.

COLOR THE PICTURE

See Them Standing Tall and Proud, Surrounded by A Heart Shaped **"SAFETY BUBBLE"**

CHAPTER 2:
MY BODY, MY BOUNDARIES

WHY ARE BOUNDARIES IMPORTANT?

Boundaries are like invisible fences that help keep us safe and comfortable. They protect our bodies, our feelings, and our personal space. Just like how a fence around a yard keeps the people inside safe and keeps others from coming in without permission, personal boundaries do the same thing for our bodies and emotions.

Here are some reasons why boundaries are important:

1. **Safety:** Boundaries help keep you safe by letting others know what you are and aren't okay with. This can include physical touches, sharing personal information, or anything else that makes you feel uncomfortable.

2. **Respect:** When you set boundaries, you're showing respect for yourself and your needs. You're telling others that your feelings and choices matter. Respecting others' boundaries shows that you care about their well-being too.

3. **Healthy Relationships:** Having clear boundaries helps create healthy relationships with friends, family, and others. When everyone understands and respects each other's limits, it builds trust and makes people feel valued.

4. **Confidence:** Setting boundaries can help you feel more confident and in control of your life. You'll know what you stand for and what you won't accept from others.

5. **Personal Space:** Boundaries give you the space you need to feel comfortable and secure. This can be physical space, like not wanting someone to stand too close, or emotional space, like needing time alone when you feel upset.

Remember, your boundaries matter, and it's okay to say "no" to things that make you uncomfortable. If someone doesn't respect your boundaries, tell a trusted adult who can help you. And always make sure to respect other people's boundaries, too!

PART 1: MY SAFE ZONES

COLOR YOUR SAFE ZONES

On the picture of the body on the next page, color the areas that you feel comfortable with people touching, like your hands or shoulders. Remember, it's okay to say no to any touch that makes you feel uncomfortable.

Discussion Questions:
- What areas did you color?
- Why do you feel comfortable with people touching these areas?
- Are there any areas you did not color?
- Why do you feel these areas are private?

PART 2: USING THE RIGHT WORDS

LEARN THE NAMES

Match the correct anatomical terms to the body parts. Draw a line from each word to the right spot on the body outline.

- Head
- Hand
- Chest
- Nipples
- Penis (for boys)
- Anus
- Arm
- Foot
- Breasts
- Stomach
- Vagina (for girls)
- Understanding Different Terms

Different cultures and families may use different terms for body parts, and that's okay! What's important is that everyone in your family understands what terms are being used.

Write down the terms you and your trusted adult agree to use:

Head: _____

Arm: _____

Hand: _____

Leg: _____

Foot: _____

Chest: _____

Stomach: _____

Breasts: _____

Nipples: _____

Penis (boys): _____

Vagina (girls): _____

Anus: _____

Discussion Questions:
- Why is it important for everyone in our family to use the same words for body parts?
- How does knowing the right names help us stay safe?

PART 3: MY BOUNDARIES RULES

DRAW YOUR BOUNDARY CIRCLE

Draw a circle around the body outline showing your personal boundary space. This is the space where you decide who can come close.

Discussion Questions:

- Who do you feel comfortable having inside your boundary circle? Why?
- What should you do if someone you don't feel comfortable with tries to come inside your boundary circle?

Head

Arm

Hand

Foot

Chest

Breasts

Nipples

Stomach

Penis (for boys)

Vagina (for girls)

Anus

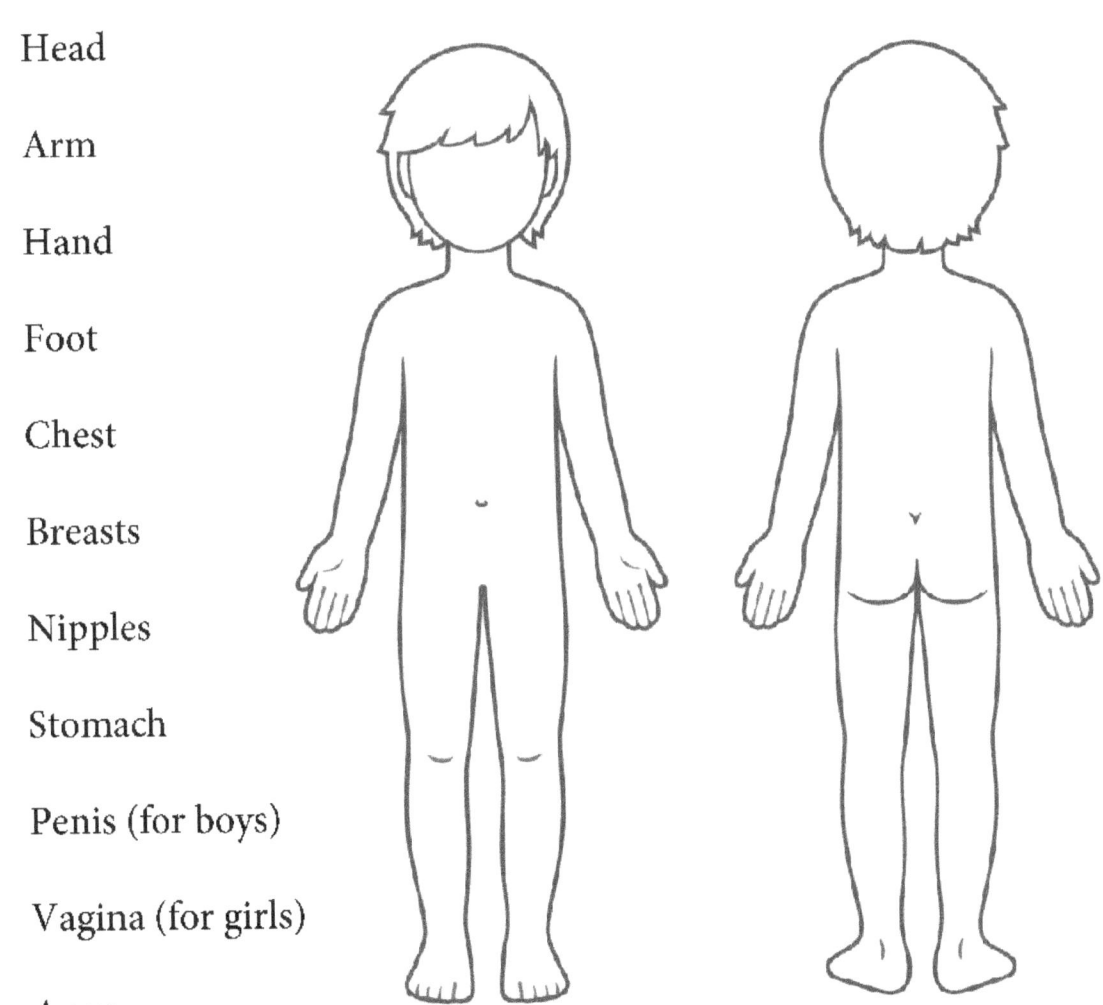

THINKING ABOUT DIFFERENT TYPES OF TOUCH

Touch is one of the ways we interact with the world around us. Some touches feel good, while others might make us feel uncomfortable or confused. It's important to understand how different types of touch make you feel.

Now, let's think about each type of touch:

1. **Safe Touches:** These are touches that make you feel happy, loved, and cared for. They might include hugs from your parents, high fives from your friends, or a pat on the back from your teacher when you do a good job.

   - How do safe touches make you feel inside?
   - Can you think of some examples of safe touches in your life?

2. **Unsafe Touches:** These are touches that hurt you or make you feel scared or uncomfortable. They might include hitting, kicking, or touching your private parts (the parts of your body covered by a swimsuit).

   - How do you think unsafe touches might make someone feel?
   - What should you do if someone gives you an unsafe touch?

3. **Confusing Touches:** These are touches that don't necessarily hurt, but they still make you feel weird, mixed-up, or unsure inside. They could be a hug that lasts too long, tickling that doesn't

stop when you ask, or someone touching you in a way that makes you feel funny or strange.

- How might confusing touches make you feel?
- What can you do if you get a confusing touch?

Remember, your body belongs to you, and you have the right to say "no" to any touch that makes you feel uncomfortable or confused. If you're not sure about a touch, or if it just doesn't feel right, always tell a trusted adult. They can help you understand your feelings and keep you safe.

Take a look at the chart below. It shows different types of touch: SAFE TOUCHES, UNSAFE TOUCHES AND CONFUSING TOUCHES.

Type of Touch	Examples
Good Touch	Hugging a family member or close friend High fives or handshakes A pat on the back from a coach or teacher Holding hands with a parent or guardian Getting help from a doctor during a medical check-up
Bad Touch	Touching private parts (unless for medical reasons) Unwanted hug or kisses Being touched by a stranger Being forced to touch someone else Any touch that feels wrong or uncomfortable
Confusing Touch	Tickling that goes too far A hug from someone you don't know well A pat on the back that feels too hard Being touched by a doctor without explanation When a familiar person touches you in a new way

Take a CRAYON and CIRCLE areas where there are safe touches. Now take a crayon and make Xs where the unsafe touches are, and then make squares around areas that make you feel unsure or confused and you can talk about that with your trusted adult.

Grab your CRAYONS and get ready to COLOR along as
we read the story together!

MY BODY, MY BOUNDARIES

In a small, friendly town where the sun always shines,
Lived two young friends who had wonderful times.
Bobby, with his bright blue eyes and hair of brown,
And Suzi, with golden curls and a smile that never frowns.

They played in the park, ran through fields wide and green,
Exploring the world, so much to be seen.
But one thing they learned, both Bobby and Suzi,
Was the importance of boundaries, for you and for me?
One day in the park, they met Mrs. Owl,
A wise old bird, with a face so solemn and foul.
She said, "Listen closely, dear Bobby and Suzi,
For knowing your boundaries is essential, truly."

"If someone gets too close and it doesn't feel right,
It's okay to say no, with all of you might.
Your body is yours, from your head to your toe,
And setting boundaries is the way you should go."

Bobby looked at Suzi, and Suzi at him,
They knew that their lesson must start from within.
Suzi spoke first, her voice strong and clear,
"My body is mine; I will make that known here."

Bobby nodded and added, with a confident grin,
"No one can touch me without my permission within.
I'll speak up for myself, and protect what I treasure,
I'm in charge of my own body, and that makes me feel safe and
strong."

Bobby nodded and added, with a confident grin,
"No one can touch me without my permission within.
I'll speak up for myself, and protect what I treasure,
I'm in charge of my own body, and that makes me feel safe and strong."

In their adventures, through the woods and the streams,
They taught their friends about boundaries and the freedom it gives to be who you are!
To stand up tall, and say what they feel,
To make sure their spaces are respected and real.

One sunny morning, while at school to learn,
A new friend named Jamie, with concern, took a turn.
"Can I hug you, Suzi? Is that alright?"
Suzi smiled and said, "Thank you for asking, that's polite."

Jamie then asked Bobby, "May I hold your hand?"
Bobby replied, "No thanks, but I understand."
They shared with Jamie the lessons they knew,
About personal space and respect that grew.

And so, the story of Bobby and Suzi,
Spread through the town, making everyone cozy.
They knew that their bodies were theirs to protect,
And respecting each other was a sign of respect.

From that day forward, in that sunshiny town,
Boundaries were honored, no one felt down.
For everyone knew, young and old,
That their bodies were precious, a truth to be told.

So, remember the tale of Bobby and Suzi,
And the wise old Mrs. Owl, so truthful and choosy.
Your body is yours, from head to toe,
Respect your boundaries, and let others know.

CHAPTER 3:
I CAN SAY "NO"

IT'S OKAY TO SAY "NO"

Your body belongs to you, and you have the right to say "no" to any touch that makes you feel uncomfortable, scared, or confused. It doesn't matter if it's a friend, a family member, or someone you don't know well – if a touch doesn't feel right, you can say "no."

HOW TO SAY "NO"

When you need to say "no" to an uncomfortable touch, remember these tips:

1. Stand tall and look the person in the eye. Show them that you mean what you say.
2. Use a strong, clear voice. Say "No" loudly enough for the person to hear you.
3. Use firm words. Say something like: "No, I don't like that." "No, please stop." "No, that makes me feel uncomfortable."
4. Move away from the situation if you can. Take a step back or go to a different room.
5. Tell a trusted adult. If the person doesn't listen to your "no," find an adult you trust and tell them what happened.

Remember, you don't have to explain or apologize for saying "no." Your feelings are important, and you have the right to set boundaries.

WHY SAYING "NO" IS IMPORTANT

Saying "no" to uncomfortable touches is important because:

1. It protects your personal space. Your body is yours, and you get to decide who touches you and how.
2. It shows self-respect. When you say "no," you're standing up for yourself and your feelings.
3. It communicates your boundaries. Saying "no" helps others understand what you are and aren't okay with.
4. It keeps you safe. If a touch makes you feel scared or uncomfortable, saying "no" can help you get out of the situation.

Practice saying "no" in different ways, like using a serious face or a firm voice. You can even roleplay with a trusted adult to get more comfortable saying "no."

Always Remember: if someone doesn't listen to your "no" or keeps touching you in a way that makes you feel uncomfortable, it's not your fault. Tell a trusted adult right away so they can help keep you safe.

Practice saying no by writing "NO" in the bubble. Practice saying "no" and asking for help in different situations. How does it make you feel to say no and to set a boundary?

CHAPTER 4:
MY FEELINGS AND EMOTIONS MATTER

RECOGNIZING EMOTIONS

Emotions are feelings that we have inside us. They can be big or small, and they can change depending on what's happening around us. It's important to know how to recognize and name your emotions so you can understand them better.

Here are some common emotions:

- **Happy:** When you feel good inside and want to smile or laugh. You might feel happy when you play with friends, get a hug from someone you love, or do something fun.

- **Sad:** When you feel down or low inside and might want to cry. You might feel sad when you miss someone, lose something important to you, or when something doesn't go the way, you wanted.

- **Scared:** When you feel afraid or like you might be in danger. You might feel scared when you're in a new place, when you hear a loud noise, or when something happens that you don't expect.

- **Angry:** When something makes you feel upset or mad inside. You might feel angry when someone takes your toy, when you can't do something, you want to do, or when things feel unfair.

- **Confused:** When you feel mixed-up or unsure inside. You might feel confused when you don't understand something, when someone says or does something that doesn't make sense to you, or when you have a problem, you don't know how to solve.

It's okay to feel all of these emotions and more. Everyone feels different emotions at different times. The important thing is to pay attention to your feelings and talk about them with someone you trust.

Color each section of the wheel a different color, based on the emotion it represents to you.

For Example:

Red for angry   Blue for sad

Yellow for happy   Green for calm

Purple for scared   Orange for confused

- Can you think about times when you have felt each emotion?
- How did you express those feelings?

Here are some ways you can move your body when you have these feelings and emotions.

Angry: Take deep breaths, talk to an adult, draw a picture

Sad: Talk to a friend, write in a journal, hug a stuffed animal

Happy: Smile, share with others, do a happy dance

Calm: Take a break, read a book, stretch

Scared: Talk to a trusted adult, hold a comforting object, imagine a safe place

Confused: Ask questions, talk to a trusted adult, take a few deep breaths to clear your mind.

"EMOTION WHEEL" activity. This activity allows us to identify and color – code different emotions. We can think about how they can express those feelings in healthy ways.

MINDFULNESS AND MEDITATION

Sit quietly and focus on your breathing. Think about how your body feels.

Are you Happy, Sad, or Something Else?
It is good to check in with how you are feeling

TRUSTING YOUR INSTINCTS

Your instincts are the little voice inside you that tells you when something feels right or wrong. It's like a special helper that keeps you safe. Trusting your instincts means listening to that little voice and paying attention to how your body feels.

Here are some ways your instincts might tell you that something isn't right:

- You get a funny feeling in your tummy, like butterflies or knots.
- Your heart beats faster or your hands feel sweaty.
- You feel like you want to hide or run away.
- You have a little voice inside telling you "No" or "Stop."

If you ever get these feelings, especially when it comes to touches or situations with other people, it's important to trust your instincts. Even if you're not sure why something feels wrong, your instincts are trying to keep you safe.

When you trust your instincts, you can:

- Say "no" to touches or situations that make you feel uncomfortable.
- Move away from people or places that don't feel safe.
- Tell a trusted adult about what happened and how you feel.

Remember, your feelings are important, and you deserve to feel safe and comfortable. If something doesn't feel right, trust your instincts and talk to a grown-up you trust. They can help you understand your feelings and keep you safe.

HOW TO EXPRESS YOUR FEELINGS

Expressing your feelings can help you feel better and make sure that others understand what you're going through.

Here are some ways to express your feelings:

1. Talk to someone you trust
   - Find a grown-up you trust, like a parent, teacher, or counselor, and tell them how you feel.
   - Use "I" statements to describe your emotions, like "I feel sad because..." or "I feel angry when..."
   - Remember, it's okay to ask for help when you need it.

2. Write or draw about your feelings
   - Sometimes, it's easier to express yourself through writing or art.
   - You can keep a journal and write about your feelings each day.
   - Draw a picture that shows how you feel inside. Use colors and shapes to represent your emotions.
   - Writing and drawing can help you understand your feelings better and feel more in control.

3. Take deep breaths to help calm down
   - When you're feeling strong emotions, your body might feel tense or shaky.
   - Taking deep breaths can help you relax and feel more in control.
   - Try this: breathe in slowly through your nose for a count of four, then breathe out slowly through your mouth for a count of four. Repeat this a few times until you feel calmer.

4. Use "Calm Down Strategies" that work for you
- Different things work for different people when it comes to managing big feelings.
- Some kids like to take a break and have some quiet time alone.
- Others might want to run around outside, punch a pillow, or listen to music.
- Experiment with different activities and find what helps you feel better when you're upset.

5. Practice expressing your feelings in a safe way
- It's okay to have strong feelings, but it's not okay to hurt yourself, others, or property.
- Practice using words to express yourself, even when you're angry or upset.
- If you're feeling too overwhelmed to talk, try one of the other strategies first, like deep breathing or drawing, until you feel ready to express yourself calmly.

Remember, all of your feelings are valid, and it's important to express them in a healthy way. If you're ever unsure about how to handle your emotions, talk to a trusted adult. They can help you find ways to express yourself and feel better.

With practice and support, you'll get better at recognizing and expressing your feelings in ways that work for you. This is an important skill that will help you throughout your life!

CHAPTER 5:
MY TRUSTED ADULTS

UNDERSTANDING TRAUMA IN CHILDREN

Children who experience trauma, whether through direct events like accidents or abuse, or indirect experiences such as witnessing violence or natural disasters, can suffer significant emotional and psychological impacts. Without appropriate intervention, these impacts can lead to long-term mental health issues, including post-traumatic stress disorder (PTSD), depression, anxiety, and behavioral problems.

THE ROLE OF PARENTS AND TRUSTED ADULTS

Parents and trusted adults play a critical role in mitigating the effects of trauma on children. Immediate and consistent support can make a significant difference in a child's ability to recover and thrive. Here are key reasons why early and ongoing intervention is essential:

IMMEDIATE IMPACT REDUCTION

- Early intervention helps reduce the immediate emotional distress and confusion children may feel after a traumatic event.
- Techniques like Trauma-Focused Cognitive Behavioral Therapy (TF-CBT) have been proven effective in alleviating symptoms when started soon after the trauma.

PREVENTING LONG-TERM EFFECTS

- Addressing trauma early can prevent the development of severe and chronic mental health issues.
- Children who receive timely support are less likely to suffer from prolonged PTSD, depression, and anxiety.

BUILDING RESILIENCE

- Ongoing support helps children build resilience, enabling them to cope better with future challenges.

- Parental involvement in therapeutic processes reinforces a child's sense of security and stability.

ENHANCING EMOTIONAL PROCESSING

- Structured interventions, such as narrative exposure and cognitive restructuring, help children make sense of their experiences, reducing feelings of self-blame and confusion.

- Play therapy and other creative methods provide younger children with appropriate ways to express and process their emotions.

CREATING A SUPPORTIVE ENVIRONMENT

- A consistent, supportive response from parents and trusted adults fosters a safe environment for children to heal.

- Schools and communities can also play a vital role by implementing trauma-informed practices and providing access to mental health resources.

KEY INTERVENTIONS AND STRATEGIES

1. **Trauma-Focused Cognitive Behavioral Therapy (TF-CBT)**

- Structured, short-term therapy that significantly reduces trauma symptoms.

- Involves psychoeducation, relaxation techniques, and cognitive coping strategies.

2. **Parental Support and Training**

- Training programs for parents on trauma-informed parenting can enhance their ability to support their child effectively.

- Encouraging open communication and validating the child's feelings are crucial practices.

3. **Narrative Exposure and Cognitive Restructuring**
- Helping children create a coherent narrative of their trauma aids in emotional processing.
- Cognitive restructuring helps children replace negative thoughts with more positive, realistic ones.

4. **Play Therapy and Peer Support**
- Play therapy provides younger children with a natural way to express their emotions.
- Peer support programs help children feel less isolated and more understood.

Recommendations for Parents and Trusted Adults

- **Act Quickly:** Seek professional help as soon as possible after a traumatic event.
- **Be Consistent:** Provide ongoing support and maintain open lines of communication.
- **Educate Yourself:** Learn about trauma and its effects to better understand and support your child.
- **Create Stability:** Maintain routines and a safe environment to foster a sense of normalcy and security.
- **Collaborate with Professionals:** Work with therapists, school counselors, and other professionals to provide comprehensive support.

Early and ongoing intervention is crucial in preventing the full impact of trauma on children. By understanding the importance of timely support and utilizing effective strategies, parents and trusted adults can help children navigate their recovery journey, building resilience and fostering long-term emotional well-being.

WHO ARE TRUSTED ADULTS?

Trusted adults are grown-ups who make you feel safe, cared for, and listened to. They are people you can go to when you need help, have a problem, or just want to talk. Trusted adults can be different for everyone, but they should always be people who have your best interests at heart. In addition, if a good rule to remember is if a stranger approach you beware, but if you are in danger its ok to find an adult to help you when you need the help.

Some examples of trusted adults might be:
- Parents or guardians
- Grandparents or other family members
- Teachers or school counselors
- Coaches or activity leaders
- Family friends or neighbors you know well
- Doctors or nurses

IDENTIFYING TRUSTED ADULTS

It's important to think about who your trusted adults are before you need their help. That way, you'll know exactly who to go to when you have a problem or need to talk.

Here are some questions to help you identify your trusted adults:
- Who makes you feel safe and loved?
- Who listens to you and takes your feelings seriously?
- Who can you talk to about anything, even if it's hard or scary?
- Who helps you solve problems and make good decisions?
- Who do you trust to keep you safe and give you good advice?

Once you've thought about these questions, make a list of your trusted adults. You can write their names, draw pictures of them, or even make a special card for each one. Keep your list somewhere safe, so you can always remember who your trusted adults are.

WHY TRUSTED ADULTS ARE IMPORTANT

Having trusted adults in your life is very important. They can help you in many ways, such as:

1. **Keeping You Safe:** Trusted adults can help protect you from harm and make sure you're safe and l40 lthy.
2. **Giving You Advice:** When you have a problem or a tough decision to make, trusted adults can give you advice and help you think through your options.
3. **Helping You Solve Problems:** If you're facing a challenge or a difficult situation, trusted adults can help you find solutions and work through the problem.
4. **Listening To You:** Trusted adults are always ready to listen when you need to talk. They can help you understand and express your feelings, and they won't judge you.
5. **Supporting You:** Trusted adults are there to cheer you on, celebrate your successes, and help you learn from your mistakes. They want what's best for you and will support you through good times and bad.

Remember, if you ever feel unsafe, scared, or unsure about something, your trusted adults are there to help. Don't be afraid to talk to them, even if it's about something difficult or embarrassing. They care about you and want to make sure you're okay.

If you ever tell a trusted adult about a problem and they don't listen or help, don't give up. Keep telling trusted adults until you get the help you need. Your safety and well-being are very important! We will now select some trusted adults!

It is time to find **TWO** or **THREE** trusted adults who will promise to always listen and to believe you, have them read to you the contract and you both can sign!

MY SAFETY RULES

I, _____ (child's name), and my trusted adult,
_____ (trusted adult's name), promise to follow
these rules to keep me safe:

1. My body belongs to me. I can say "no" to touches that make me feel bad or scared.

2. I will tell my trusted adult if something feels wrong, even if someone says it's a secret.

3. There are good touches, bad touches, and confusing touches. I will tell my trusted adult if I get a bad or confusing touch.

4. Some secrets are okay, but I will tell my trusted adult about secrets that make me feel bad or worried.

5. It's never my fault if someone tries to hurt me or make me feel bad.

6. If I need help, I will talk to my trusted adult or another safe grown-up.

As The Trusted Adult, I Promise To:
1. Listen to and believe the child.

2. Help the child understand that it's not their fault if someone hurts them.

3. Make sure the child feels safe talking to me.

4. Help the child if they tell me about something bad happening to them.

5. Teach the child about staying safe.
   **We both sign this to show that we will work together to keep the child safe and happy. **

_____

Child's Signature   Trusted Adult's Signature

_____

Date   Date

MY SAFETY RULES

I, _____ (child's name), and my trusted adult, _____ (trusted adult's name), promise to follow these rules to keep me safe:

1. My body belongs to me. I can say "no" to touches that make me feel bad or scared.

2. I will tell my trusted adult if something feels wrong, even if someone says it's a secret.

3. There are good touches, bad touches, and confusing touches. I will tell my trusted adult if I get a bad or confusing touch.

4. Some secrets are okay, but I will tell my trusted adult about secrets that make me feel bad or worried.

5. It's never my fault if someone tries to hurt me or make me feel bad.

6. If I need help, I will talk to my trusted adult or another safe grown-up.

As the trusted adult, I promise to:
1. Listen to and believe the child.

2. Help the child understand that it's not their fault if someone hurts them.
3. Make sure the child feels safe talking to me.

4. Help the child if they tell me about something bad happening to them.

5. Teach the child about staying safe.
   **We both sign this to show that we will work together to keep the child safe and happy. **

_____

Child's Signature

_____

Trusted Adult's Signature

_____

Date

_____

Date

MY SAFETY RULES

I, _____ (child's name), and my trusted adult, _____ (trusted adult's name), promise to follow these rules to keep me safe:

1. My body belongs to me. I can say "no" to touches that make me feel bad or scared.

2. I will tell my trusted adult if something feels wrong, even if someone says it's a secret.

3. There are good touches, bad touches, and confusing touches. I will tell my trusted adult if I get a bad or confusing touch.

4. Some secrets are okay, but I will tell my trusted adult about secrets that make me feel bad or worried.

5. It's never my fault if someone tries to hurt me or make me feel bad.

6. If I need help, I will talk to my trusted adult or another safe grown-up.

As the trusted adult, I promise to:
1. Listen to and believe the child.

2. Help the child understand that it's not their fault if someone hurts them.

3. Make sure the child feels safe talking to me.

4. Help the child if they tell me about something bad happening to them.

5. Teach the child about staying safe.
   **We both sign this to show t' 46 we will work together to keep the child safe and happy. **

_____   _____
Child's Signature   Trusted Adult's Signature

_____   _____
Date   Date

Here's a worksheet you should use to help children create a trusted password for when they are getting picked up by someone other than their parent or guardian:

TRUSTED PASSWORD WORKSHEET

Sometimes, your parent or guardian might ask someone else to pick you up from school, a friend's house, or another place. To make sure you stay safe, you can create a special password with your parent or guardian. This password is a secret code that only you, your parent or guardian, and the person picking you up will know.

Here's how to create your trusted password:

1. Choose a word or phrase that is easy for you to remember but hard for others to guess. It can be silly, like a funny nickname or a favorite food.
2. **Write your password here:** _____
3. Practice saying your password with your parent or guardian.
4. Your parent or guardian will make sure that the person picking you up knows the password.
5. When the person comes to pick you up, ask them for the password before going with them.
6. If the person does not know the password, do not go with them. Instead, find a trusted adult, like a teacher or a police officer, and tell them that you need help.
7. Never share your personal Password with anyone other than your parent or guardian.

Remember, your safety is very important! If you ever feel unsure or uncomfortable about someone trying to pick you up, even if they know the password, always trust your feelings and find a trusted adult to help you. Another Really important skill is memorizing the street address and your parents phone number.

Parent/Guardian Signature: _____

Child Signature: _____

Date: _____

RESOURCES

The websites and URLs mentioned in this book are provided solely as informational resources for readers who wish to further explore the topics discussed. Their inclusion does not constitute an endorsement by the author or publisher. We do not guarantee the accuracy, completeness, or timeliness of the information found on these websites. Readers are advised to use their own discretion when accessing these resources and to independently verify any information obtained from them. The author and publisher are not responsible for the content, privacy practices, or security measures of any external websites. Access to and use of these websites is at the reader's own risk.

RESOURCES

HOTLINES, HELPLINES, AND FURTHER LEARNING
- List of hotlines and helplines for children.
- Recommended books and websites for further learning.

DISCUSSING PERSONAL SAFETY
- Tips for discussing personal safety with children.
- Create a safe environment for open communication.

CREATING A SUPPORTIVE ENVIRONMENT
- How to use the coloring book as a tool for ongoing conversations.
- Encouraging children to express their thoughts and feelings.

SIGNS OF ABUSE AND HOW TO RESPOND
- Information on recognizing signs of abuse.
- Steps to take if a child discloses abuse.

ADDITIONAL RESOURCES
- List of resources for further education and support services.

EDUCATION AND PREVENTION RESOURCES

1. **Darkness to Light:** This organization is dedicated to preventing child sexual abuse. They offer training programs such as "Stewards of Children" which educates adults on how to prevent, recognize, and react responsibly to child sexual abuse. Visit [Darkness to Light] (https://www.d2l.org) for more information.

2. **RAINN (Rape, Abuse & Incest National Network):** RAINN operates the National Sexual Assault Hotline and provides extensive resources on sexual abuse prevention and response. They offer educational programs and support services for survivors of sexual abuse. Learn more at [RAINN] (https://www.rainn.org).

3. **Stop It Now:** This organization provides resources to prevent the sexual abuse of children by mobilizing adults, families, and communities. They offer educational materials, prevention programs, and a confidential helpline for those concerned about sexual abuse. More details can be found at [Stop It Now!] (https://www.stopitnow.org).

SUPPORT SERVICES

1. **National Center for Missing & Exploited Children (NCMEC):** NCMEC provides support to families and law enforcement in cases of child abduction and exploitation. They offer a CyberTipline for reporting child sexual exploitation and educational resources for preventing abuse. Visit [NCMEC] (https://www.missingkids.org) for more information.

2. **The National Child Traumatic Stress Network (NCTSN):** NCTSN offers resources and support for children who have experienced trauma, including sexual abuse. They provide training for professionals and information for families on how to help children recover from traumatic experiences. Learn more at [NCTSN] (https://www.nctsn.org).

3. **Child Help:** In addition to their broader child abuse prevention efforts, Child help provides specific resources and support for victims of child sexual abuse. Their National Child Abuse Hotline (1-800-4-A-CHILD) is available for immediate assistance. More information is available at [Child help] (https://www.childhelp.org).

IMMEDIATE HELP

1. **National Sexual Assault Hotline (RAINN):** Available 24/7, this hotline offers confidential support and resources for survivors of sexual abuse. Call 1-800-656-HOPE or visit [RAINN Hotline] (https://www.rainn.org/get-help/national-sexual-assault-hotline).

2. **Child help National Child Abuse Hotline:** Provides crisis intervention, information, and referrals to thousands of emergencies, social service, and support resources. Call 1-800-4-A-CHILD or visit [Child help Hotline] (https://www.childhelphotline.org).

3. **Stop It Now! Helpline:** Offers confidential support and resources for those concerned about child sexual abuse. Call 1-888-PREVENT or visit [Stop It Now! Helpline] (https:// www.stopitnow.org/help-guidance/helpline).

TOUCH SCENARIOS: WHAT WOULD YOU DO?

MATERIALS:

- Printable worksheets with scenario and questions
- Coloring materials (crayons, markers, or colored pencils)

INSTRUCTIONS:

1. Begin by reviewing the definitions of safe, unsafe, and confusing touches with the children.

2. Distribute the printable worksheets to each child. The worksheets should include a series of scenarios, each followed by questions and space for the child to respond.

3. Read each scenario aloud and ask the children to follow along on their worksheets. After each scenario, give the children time to think about their responses and write or draw their answers on the worksheet.

4. Encourage the children to color a green circle for safe touches, a red circle for unsafe touches, and a yellow circle for confusing touches next to each scenario.

5. Here are some sample scenarios and questions for the worksheet:
   Scenario 1: Your aunt comes to visit and gives you a big hug when she sees you.
   - Is this a safe, unsafe, or confusing touch? (Color the Circle)
   - How does this touch make you feel?

Scenario 2: A kid at the playground pushes you down and laughs.

- Is this a safe, unsafe, or confusing touch? (Color the Circle)
- How does this touch make you feel?

Scenario 3: Your coach pats you on the back after you score a goal.

- Is this a safe, unsafe, or confusing touch? (Color the Circle)
- How does this touch make you feel?

Scenario 4: Someone you don't know well wants to hold your hand, and it makes you feel weird.

- Is this a safe, unsafe, or confusing touch? (Color the Circle)
- How does this touch make you feel?

6. After the children complete their worksheets, gather the group together to discuss their responses. Encourage them to share their thoughts and feelings about each scenario.

7. Reinforce key messages throughout the discussion, such as:
   - Safe touches make us feel happy, loved, and cared for.
   - Unsafe touches hurt us or make us feel scared or uncomfortable.
   - Confusing touches make us feel weird, mixes-up, or unsure.
   - It's okay to say "no" to touches that don't feel right.
   - Always tell a trusted adult about unsafe or confusing touches.

8. Conclude the exercise by reminding the children that they can always come to you or another trusted adult if they have questions or want to talk about touches, they've experienced.

This exercise allows children to engage with the concept of different types of touch in a hands-on way, applying their understanding to specific scenarios and practicing their problem – solving skills. The worksheet format and coloring activity make the exercise more interactive and age – appropriate for 5–11 years old.

TOUCH SCENARIOS: WHAT WOULD YOU DO?

1. Introduce the concept of safe, unsafe and confusing touches using the definitions from the previous discussion.

2. Present the children with a series of scenarios involving different types of touch. For each scenario, ask the children to identify whether it represents a safe, unsafe or confusing touch and discuss how they might respond.

3. Here are some sample scenarios:
   - Your best friend gives you a high – five after you win a game together. (Safe touch)
   - A grown – up you don't know well tries to hug you and it makes you feel weird. (Confusing touch)
   - Your older sibling hits you when they get angry. (Unsafe touch)
   - Your grandparent gives you a kiss on the cheek when they see you. (Safe touch)
   - Someone at school keeps touching your hair, even after you ask them stop.
   - A babysitter wants to play a touching game that makes you feel uncomfortable. (Unsafe touch)

4. After presenting each scenario, ask the children to raise their hands or use color-coded cards to indicate whether they think it's safe, unsafe, or confusing touch.

5. Encourage discussion by asking questions like:
   - Why do you think this is a safe/unsafe/confusing touch?
   - How might this touch make someone feel?
   - What could you say or do in this situation?
   - Who could you tell if this happened to you?

6. Reinforce key messages throughout the exercise, such as:
   - You have the right to say "no" to any touch that makes you feel uncomfortable or confused.
   - Always tell a trusted adult if someone gives you an unsafe or confusing touch.
   - It's never your fault if someone touches you in a way that's not okay.

7. Conclude the exercise by reminding children that they can always talk to you or another trusted adult if they have questions or concerns about different types of touch.

This exercise allows children to apply their understanding of safe, unsafe, and confusing touches to real life scenarios, practice problem – solving skills, and discuss their feelings in a supportive environment. Adapt the scenarios as needed to ensure they are age-appropriate and relevant to the children's experiences.

Here's an exercise that reinforce the concepts of recognizing emotions and trusting instincts:

EMOTION CHARADES AND INSTINCT CHECK

MATERIALS:

1. Emotion cards (each card has an emotion word or picture, such as happy, sad, scared, angry, confused)
2. Instinct scenario cards (each card describes a situation where a child might need to trust their instincts)

INSTRUCTIONS:

1. Begin by reviewing the different emotions and the importance of trusting instincts with the children.

2. Divide the children into small groups or pairs.

3. Emotion Charades:
   - Give each group a set of emotion cards.
   - Have the children take turns picking a card and acting out the emotion for their group to guess.
   - Encourage the children to discuss times when they felt that emotion and how they expressed it.

4. Instinct Check:
   - Give each group a set of instinct scenario cards.
   - Have the children take turns picking a card and reading the scenario aloud to their group.
   - Ask the children to discuss how they might feel in that situation and what their instincts might be telling them.
   - Encourage the children to brainstorm what they could do to trust their instincts and stay safe in each scenario.

5. After the groups have finished the Emotion Charades and Instinct Check activities, bring everyone back together to discuss their experiences.

6. Ask the children to share:
    *   What they learned about recognizing emotions in themselves and others.
    *   Times when they've had to trust their instincts in real life.
    *   What they would do if they ever felt uncomfortable or unsafe in a situation.

7. Reinforce key messages throughout the discussion, such as:
    *   It's important to pay attention to your emotions and talk about them with someone you trust.
    *   Your instincts are there to help keep you safe.
    *   If something doesn't feel right, trust your instincts and tell a trusted adult.

8. Conclude the exercise by reminding the children that they can always come to you or another trusted adult if they need help understanding their emotions or if they ever feel unsafe.

This exercise combines physical activity, role-play, and discussion to help children practice recognizing emotions and trusting their instincts in a fun and engaging way. By acting out emotions and discussing scenarios where they might need to trust their instincts, children can develop a stronger understanding of these important concepts and how to apply them in their daily lives.

Here's an expanded version of the Emotion Wheel coloring exercise, with more detailed instructions and additional discussion points:

MATERIALS:

Printed Emotion Wheel worksheets (a circular diagram divided into sections, with each section representing a different emotion) Coloring materials (crayons, markers, or colored pencils)

INSTRUCTIONS:

1. Begin by discussing the importance of recognizing and expressing feelings with the children. Explain that everyone experiences a wide range of emotions, and it's essential to find healthy ways to express them.

2. Distribute the Emotion Wheel worksheets and coloring materials to each child. Explain that each section of the wheel represents a different emotion, and they will be coloring each section a different color.

3. Ask the children to color each section of the wheel a different color, based on the emotion it represents. Suggest colors for each emotion, but allow the children to choose their own if they prefer. For Example:
   - Red for angry
   - Blue for sad
   - Yellow for happy
   - Green for calm
   - Purple for scared
   - Orange for confused

4. As the children color, encourage them to think about times when they've felt each emotion. Ask them to consider what triggered those feelings and how they expressed them. Remind them that all feelings are valid, and it's okay to experience a range of emotions.

5. Once the children have finished coloring their Emotion Wheels, have them write or draw ways they can express each emotion in a healthy way next to the corresponding section. Encourage them to think of multiple strategies for each emotion. For Example:
    - **Angry:** Take deep breaths, talk to an adult, draw a picture, go for a walk, do something physical
    - **Sad:** Talk to a friend, write in a journal, hug a stuffed animal, listen to music, do something comforting
    - **Happy:** Smile, share with others, do a happy dance, make someone else smile, celebrate
    - **Calm:** Take a break, read a book, stretch, do a puzzle, practice mindfulness
    - **Scared:** Talk to a trusted adult, hold a comforting object, imagine a safe place, do something distracting, learn about what scares you
    - **Confused:** Ask questions, talk to a teacher, take a break, look for more information, break the problem into smaller parts

6. After the children have completed their Emotion Wheels, gather the group together to discuss their ideas for expressing emotions. Encourage the children to share their completed wheels with the group.

7. Facilitate a discussion about the different emotions and expression strategies. Ask the children questions like:
    - What colors did you choose for each emotion, and why?
    - Can you share a time when you felt one of these emotions strongly?
    - Which strategies for expressing emotions do you think would work best for you?
    - Why is it important to express our emotions in healthy ways?

8. Reinforce key messages throughout the discussion, such as:
    - All feelings are valid, and it's important to express them.

    - There are many healthy ways to express emotions, and different strategies work for different people.
    - It's okay to ask for help when you're unsure how to handle your feelings.
    - Expressing emotions in healthy ways can help us feel better and understand ourselves and others better.

9. Conclude the exercise by reminding the children that they can always come to you or another trusted adult if they need help expressing or understanding their emotions. Encourage them to keep their Emotion Wheels in a safe place and refer to them when they need help identifying or expressing their feelings.

10. Consider displaying the completed Emotion Wheels in the classroom or sending them home with the children to serve as a reminder of the different emotions and healthy expression strategies.

This expanded version of the Emotion Wheel coloring exercise provides more opportunities for children to reflect on their own experiences with emotions and engage in meaningful discussions about healthy expression strategies. By exploring emotions in a creative and interactive way, children can develop a stronger understanding of their feelings and build a more comprehensive toolkit for managing them effectively.

ROLE PLAYING SCENARIOS

These exercises will help you talk through scenarios your children may encounter and will help them stay safe!

Role Play is a Powerful tool to integrate new ideas and learnings into their everyday life.

SCENARIO 1: THE UNCOMFORTABLE HUG

Role A: You are a child at a family gathering. An aunt you don't see very often comes up to you and wants to give you a big hug, but it makes you feel uncomfortable.

Role B: You are the aunt who wants to hug the child.

Practice: The child should say "No, thank you. I don't want a hug right now."

"No, thank you. I don't want a hug right now."

SCENARIO 2: THE SECRET TOUCH

Role A: You are a child playing at a friend's house. Your friend's older sibling asks you to play a special "secret" game that involves touching private parts.

Role B: You are the older sibling who is trying to convince the child to play the "secret" game.

Practice: The child should say "No" assertively, leave the situation, and tell a trusted adult.

SCENARIO 3: THE PERSISTENT STRANGER

Role A: You are a child walking home from school. A stranger approach you and asks for help finding their lost puppy. When you say "no," they keep insisting.

Role B: You are the stranger who is trying to convince the child to come with you.

Practice: The child should say "No" repeatedly, use assertive body language, and seek help from a nearby trusted adult or safe place.

SCENARIO 4: THE INAPPROPRIATE TOUCH

Role A: You are a child at a doctor's appointment. The doctor touches you in a way that makes you feel confused and uncomfortable.

Role B: You are the doctor who is inappropriately touching the child during the examination.

Practice: The child should express their discomfort, tell the doctor to stop, and report the incident to a parent or trusted adult.

SCENARIO 5: THE TRICKY BABYSITTER

Role A: You are a child being babysat by a new babysitter. The babysitter suggests playing a game that involves taking off clothes, but it makes you feel uncomfortable.

Role B: You are the babysitter who is trying to convince the child to play the inappropriate game.

Practice: The child should say "No" firmly, leave the situation, and tell their parents about what happened as soon as they return.

"No, I don't want play that game"

SCENARIO 6: THE ONLINE STRANGER

Role A: You are a child playing an online game. Another player starts asking personal questions and wants to meet up in real life.

Role B: You are the online player who is trying to convince the child to share personal information and meet in person.

Practice: The child should end the conversation, not share any personal information, and tell a parent or trusted adult about the interaction.

SCENARIO 7: THE PEER PRESSURE

Role A: You are a child at school. A group of classmates is pressuring you to do something that makes you feel uncomfortable, like stealing or bullying another student.

Role B: You are one of the classmates trying to pressure the child into participating in the inappropriate activity.

Practice: The child should say "No" assertively, suggest alternative activities, and seek help from a teacher or trusted adult if the pressure continues.